1

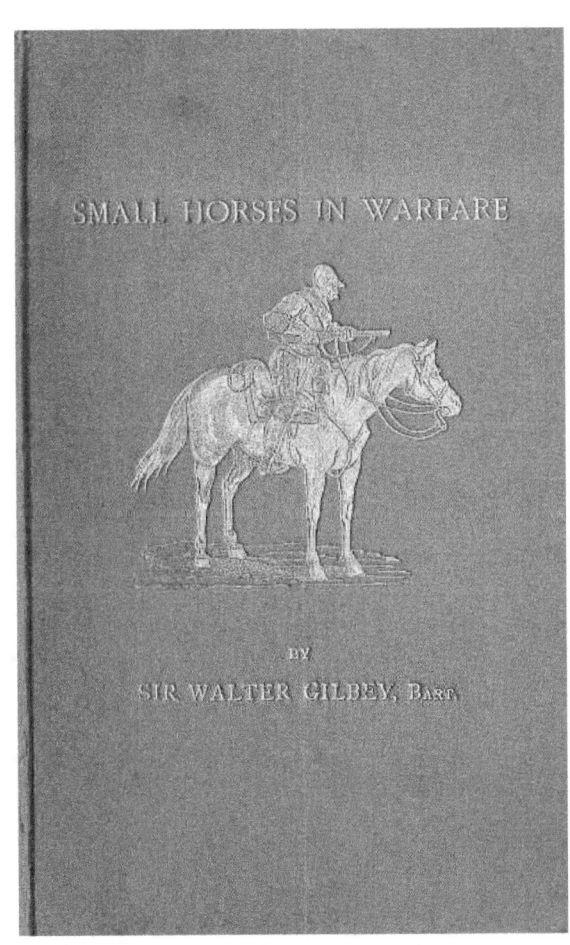

SMALL HORSES IN WARFARE

BY
SIR WALTER GILBEY, Bart.

3

The present seems an appropriate time to put forward a few facts which go to prove the peculiar suitability of small horses for certain campaigning work which demands staying power, hardiness and independence of high feeding. The circumstance that the military authorities have been obliged to look to foreign countries for supplies of such horses for the war in South Africa has suggested the propriety of pointing out that we possess in England foundation stock from which we may be able to raise a breed of small horses equal to, or better than, any we are now obliged to procure abroad.

Elsenham Hall, Essex,
May, 1900.

SMALL HORSES IN WARFARE.

The campaign in South Africa has proved beyond doubt the necessity for a strong force similar to that of the Boers. Their rapidity of movement has given us an important lesson in the military value of horses of that useful type which is suitable for light cavalry and mounted infantry.

Since the war broke out we have seen that we possess numbers of men able to ride and shoot, who only need a little training to develop them into valuable soldiers, but our difficulty throughout has been to provide horses of the stamp required for the work they have to perform. The experience we have gained in South Africa goes to confirm that acquired in the Crimea, where it was found that the horses sent out from England were unable to withstand the climate, poor food, and the hardships to which they were subjected, while the small native horses and those bred in countries further East suffered little from these causes. It was then proved beyond dispute that these small horses are both hardy and enduring, while, owing to their possession like our English thoroughbreds of a strong strain of Arab blood, they were speedy enough for light cavalry purposes.

Breeders of every class of horse, saving only those who breed the Shetland pony and the few who aim at getting ponies for polo, have for generations made it their object to obtain increased height. There is nothing to be urged against this policy in so far as certain breeds are concerned; the sixteen-hand thoroughbred with his greater stride is more likely to win races than the horse of fifteen two; the sixteen-hand carriage horse, other qualities being equal, brings a better price than one of less stature; and the Shire horse of 16.2 or 17 hands has commonly in proportion greater strength and weight, the qualities most desirable in him, than a smaller horse. Thus we can show excellent reason for our endeavours to increase the height of our most valuable breeds; and the long period that has elapsed since we were last called upon to put forward our military strength has allowed us to lose sight of the great importance of other qualities.

Breeders and horsemen are well aware, though the general public may not know or may not realise the fact, that increased height in the horse does not necessarily involve increased strength in all directions, such as greater weight-carrying power and more endurance. Granting that the saying, "a good big horse is better than a good little one," is in the main correct, we have to consider that the merits which go to make a useful horse for campaigning are infinitely more common in small horses than in big ones.

All the experience of campaigners, explorers and travellers goes to prove that small compact animals between 13.2 and 14.2 hands high are those on which reliance can be placed for hard and continuous work on scanty and innutritious food.

HORSES IN THE CRIMEAN WAR.

During the Crimean War I was located for a short time at Abydos in Asia Minor, on the shores of the Dardanelles, and had daily opportunities of seeing the horses and studying the manœuvres of some 3,000 mounted Bashi Bazouks and Armenian troops who were encamped there under General Beatson in readiness for summons to the Crimea, whither they were eventually dispatched.

The horses on which these troops were mounted ranged from 14 hands to 14.3; all had a strong strain of Arab blood, and had come with the troops from the Islands of the Archipelago. They were perfect horses for light cavalry work. The economy with which they were fed was surprising: their feed consisted principally of chopped straw with a small daily ration of barley when the grain was procurable, which was not always the case; and on this diet they continued in condition to endure long journeys which would have speedily broken down the best English charger in the British army.

CAPE HORSES.

The universal opinion of residents in South Africa is against the introduction of imported horses for general work, inasmuch as they cannot withstand the climate, hard living, bad roads and rough usage which make up the conditions of a horse's life in the Colony.

In past years, before the present war, large numbers of English horses have been sent to Natal for military service, but the results were not satisfactory; all became useless, and the large majority died; the change from English stables and English methods of management to those in vogue in the Colony almost invariably proved fatal.

BASHI BAZOUK

Some five years ago, when discussing with Mr. Cecil Rhodes the advisability of introducing into Cape Colony English sires to improve the stamp of horse bred in South Africa, he gave his opinion against such measures. He pointed out that highly bred and large horses were unsuitable for the work required in the Colony; they needed greater care in housing, feeding, and grooming than the conditions of life in South Africa would allow owners to bestow upon them. The hardships attendant upon long journeys over rough country, the extremes of heat and cold which horses must endure with insufficient shelter or none at all, must inevitably overtax the stamina which has been weakened by generations of luxurious existence in England.

Mr. Rhodes considered that no infusion of English blood would enhance the powers of the small colonial bred horse to perform the work required of him under local conditions; that though thoroughbred blood would improve him in height and speed, these advantages would be obtained at the cost of such indispensable qualities as endurance and ability to thrive on poor and scanty fare.

It is however permissible to suppose that a gradual infusion of good blood carefully chosen might in course of time benefit the Cape breed. The use only of horses which have become acclimatised would perhaps produce better results than have hitherto been obtained. The progeny reared under the ordinary conditions prevailing in the Colony would perpetuate good qualities, retaining the hardiness of the native breed.

PONIES IN THE SOUDAN.

The late Colonel P. H. S. Barrow furnished a most interesting and suggestive Report to the War Office on the Arabs which were used by his regiment, the 19th Hussars, during the Nile campaign of 1885. This report is published among the Appendices to Colonel John Biddulph's work, *The XIXth and their Times* (1899).

Experience, in the words of Colonel Biddulph, had shown that English horses could not stand hard work under a tropical sun with scarcity of water and desert fare. It was therefore decided before leaving Cairo to mount the regiment entirely on the small Syrian Arab horses used by the Egyptian cavalry. Three hundred and fifty of these little horses had been sent up in advance and were taken over by the regiment on arrival at Wady Halfa. Colonel Barrow thus describes these horses:

"Arab stallion. Average height, 14 hands; average age, 8 years to 9 years; some 15 per cent. over 12 years; bought by Egyptian Government in Syria and Lower Egypt; average price, £18."

About half of the ponies had been through the campaign in the Eastern Soudan with the regiment in February and March, 1884, and had returned in a very exhausted state. In September of that year they were marched up from Assouan to Wady Halfa, 210 miles; and when handed over to the 19th again in November, all except some 10 per cent. of the number were "in very fair marching condition." From Wady Halfa the regiment proceeded to Korti, a distance of 360 miles, at a rate of about 16 miles per day, halts, one of one day and one of two days not included; their feed consisted of about 6 lbs. of barley or dhoora[1] and 10 lbs. of dhoora stalk; and on this rather scanty ration the horses reached Korti in very good condition. Here they remained for eighteen days, receiving 8 lbs. of green dhoora stalk daily instead of 8 lbs. dry; the rest and change to green food produced improvement in their condition.

Dhoora is a kind of millet cultivated throughout Asia and introduced into the south of Europe; called also Indian millet and Guinea corn.

While the main body rested at Korti, a detachment of fifty went to Gakdul, 100 miles distant, on reconnaissance; they performed the march in sixty-three hours, had fifteen hours rest at Gakdul, and returned in the same time. Six of the party returned more rapidly, covering the 100 miles in forty-six hours, the last 50 being covered in seven and a-half hours. During these marches the horses were ridden for eighty-three hours, the remaining fifty-eight hours of the time occupied being absorbed by halts.

The reconnaissance party having returned on the 5th, the regiment, numbering 8 officers and 127 men, with 155 horses, started, on January 8, to march with General Sir Herbert Stewart's column across the desert to Gubat. This march, 336 miles, occupied from January 8 to February 20, 4 miles only being covered in the hour they were moving on the last date. They halted on the 13th at Gakdul; whereby the average day's journey works out at nearly 26 miles per day, or, if we ignore the march (4 miles in one hour) of January 20, at nearly 28 miles per day. The hardest day was the 16th, when the regiment travelled 40 miles in 11-1/2 hours, from 4.30 a.m. to 4 p.m., the horses receiving each half-a-gallon of water and 4 lbs. of food grain. Their ability to work on scanty diet was put to the test on this fortnight's march. The average daily ration for the first ten days was from 5 to 6 lbs. of grain and 2 gallons of water; the horses covering an average of 31 miles per day exclusive of the halt at Gakdul on the 13th.

When the final advance to the Nile was made, the horses went fifty-five hours with no water at all, and only 1 lb. of grain; some 15 or 20 horses were upwards of seventy hours without water. During their halt at Gubat from January 20 to February 14, they had received but one ration of grain, 6 lbs. given them two days before they had to start for the Nile. During this period they performed out-post and patrol duty averaging about 8 miles daily.

On the return march, the journey between Dongola and Wady Halfa, 250 miles, was performed on an average rate of 16 miles per day, with one two-days' halt. On this march the regiment usually travelled at night for the sake of coolness, but the scanty shade available generally compelled exposure to the hot sun all day.

Colonel Barrow remarks, "I think it may be considered a most remarkable circumstance that out of 350 horses, during nine months on a hard campaign, only twelve died from disease." Colonel Biddulph sums up the work of the horses in a few words: "The performance of the small Arab horses, both with the river and desert columns, carrying a heavy weight, on scanty fare and less water, is a marvel of endurance." The former officer attributes the small percentage of loss from disease to the facts (1) that the climate of the Soudan is most suitable for horses, (2) that the Syrian horse has a wonderful constitution, and is admirably suited for warfare in an Eastern climate. Colonel Barrow's opinion on the suitability of the Eastern climate for horses must not be read as meaning for horses of all breeds. On the contrary, Colonel Biddulph, in words quoted on a previous page, states that experience had shown that English horses could not withstand the conditions of campaigning in the Soudan.

Sir Richard Green Price, writing over the familiar pen-name of "Borderer," in *Baily's Magazine*, has urged the formation of a regiment of Lilliputian horse, to consist of men under five feet, or five feet six inches, weighing not over eleven stone, of good chest measurement: these he would mount on ponies not over 14.2 and equip with light arms and accoutrements. As he points out, increase in our cavalry is an admitted necessity, and this branch of it in particular appeals to the common sense of the people as a quick and handy service:

"After many years of practical experience of what ponies can and do accomplish, especially well-bred ones hardily reared, I do not hesitate to say that they will beat moderate horses of double their size, and that very few of our present cavalry horses could live with them in a campaign—they are more easily taught, handled and mounted than bigger horses, and with twice their constitution and thrice their sense—with riders to suit them, where are the drawbacks to their employment?"

Sir Richard, in brief, urges the creation of a regiment of scouts or mounted infantry whose horses shall be of much the same type of those described by Colonel Barrow.

The special correspondent of the *Times* with the Modder River force, in course of an article on this arm, which appears likely to play a large part in the wars of the future, writes thus of the animals used by the Colonists and Boers:—

"Here in South Africa the country-bred pony, tractable, used to fire, and taught to remain where he is left if the reins be dropped from the bit, is already a half-trained animal for these purposes, and the work of training has been slight in consequence; but in Afghanistan, and other places where the mounted infantry man has been tried in a lesser degree, the chief cause of trouble has been found in his mount."

The South African ponies ridden by the Colonial scouts and mounted infantry have acquired their education as shooting ponies on the veldt under conditions very similar to those prevailing in warfare. There is radical difference between animals so trained and ill-broken Indian country-breds whose tempers have been far too frequently spoiled by rough usage in native hands. The mounted infantry in Afghanistan might well find trouble with such ponies.

ONE OF REMINGTON'S HORSE.
Showing type of horse used by mounted infantry and scouts in the South African War.
(By permission of the Proprietors of the "Daily Graphic.")

BURNABY'S RIDE TO KHIVA.

Captain Burnaby, in his well-known book, *A Ride to Khiva*, describes the animals brought up for his inspection at Kasala, in Turkestan, when his wish to buy a horse was made known:—

"The horses were for the most part of the worst description, that is to say, as far as appearance was concerned.... Except for their excessive leanness, they looked more like huge Newfoundland dogs than as connected with the equine race, and had been turned out in the depth of winter with no other covering save the thick coats which nature had given them.... At last, after rejecting a number of jades which looked more fit to carry my boots than their wearer, I selected a little black horse. He was about 14 hands in height, and I eventually became his owner, saddle and bridle into the bargain, for the sum of £5, this being considered a very high price at Kasala."

The reader may be reminded that the winter of 1876-7, during which Captain Burnaby accomplished his adventurous journey, was an exceptionally severe one even for that part of the world, where long and severe winters are the rule. On the day of his departure from Kasala the thermometer stood at eight degrees below zero. The traveller was by no means favourably impressed with the powers of the horse he had selected as the least bad of a very poor lot, and the native guides started apparently satisfied that it would break down under its heavy rider clad to resist the penetrating cold.

After his second march, Captain Burnaby began to acquire a certain measure of respect for this pony:—

"What had surprised me most during our morning's march was the extreme endurance of our horses. The guide frequently had been obliged to dismount and to clean out their nostrils, which were entirely stuffed with icicles; but the little animals had ploughed their way steadily through the snow.... The one I rode, which in England would not have been considered able to carry my boots, was as fresh as possible after his march of seventeen miles. In spite of the weight on his back—quite twenty stone—he had never shown the least sign of fatigue."

Again, a few days later, the conditions of the journey having been no less trying:—

"From Jana Darya we rode forty miles without a halt. I must say that I was astonished to see how well the Kirghiz horses stood the long journeys. We had now gone 300 miles; and my little animal, in spite of his skeleton-like appearance, carried me quite as well as the day he left Kasala, this probably being owing to the change in his food from grass to barley. We are apt to think very highly of English horses, and deservedly as far as pace is concerned; but if it came to a question of endurance, I much doubt whether our large and well fed horses could compete with the little half-starved Kirghiz animals. This is a subject which must be borne in mind in the event of future complications in the East."

It is clear that Captain Burnaby was somewhat puzzled by the qualities displayed by a steed which looked so unpromising; he seeks to explain its performance by the better food it had enjoyed while on the march, and begins to compare the staying power of English horses with those of the Kirghiz pony with doubts as to the superiority of the former. At a later date he records without surprise that his party travelled forty miles in six hours, the horses having gone all the time at a slow steady trot. On his return journey, while staying at Petro-Alexandrovsk, he was given a mount on a little bay, hardly 14 hands high, for a day's hunting; and records that it "danced about beneath me as if he had been carrying a feather-weight jockey for the Cambridgeshire." The Kirghiz and Bokharans who accompanied him evidently thought his weight would prove too much for the pony, and when there was a ditch to be jumped looked round to see how the bay would manage it. "Never a stumble ... the hardy little beast could have carried Daniel Lambert if that worthy but obese gentleman had been resuscitated for the occasion."

Finally, Captain Burnaby sums up the performance of this fourteen-hand pony:—

"We had ridden 371 miles in exactly nine days and two hours, thus averaging more than 40 miles a day! At the same time it must be remembered that, with an interval of in all not more than nine days' rest, my horse had previously carried me 500 miles. In London, judging by his size, he would have been put down as a polo pony. In spite of the twenty stone he carried, he had never been either sick or lame during the journey, and had galloped the last 17 miles through the snow to Kasala in one hour and twenty-five minutes."

The same author describes a remarkable forced march made in the summer of 1870 by Count Borkh in Russian Tartary. The Count's mission was to test the possibility of taking artillery over the steep and difficult passes in a certain district, and his force consisted of 150 cossacks, and 60 mounted riflemen and a gun. The troops accomplished their journey out and back, 266 miles, in six days; the heat was excessive, the thermometer marking sometimes as much as 117° Fahr. during the day; yet the ponies were none the worse of their exertions, the "sick list" at the end comprising only twelve, all of which suffered from sore backs caused by careless saddling. Other expeditions under similar conditions are mentioned; these go to prove that the endurance of the Tartar pony is affected as little by heat as by cold.

POST HORSES IN SIBERIA.

Mr. H. de Windt, in his book *From Pekin to Calais*, bears witness to the wonderful endurance of the small post-horses supplied to travellers in Siberia. He describes them as very little beasts ranging from 14.2 to 15 hands. "Though rough and ungroomed, they are well fed, as they need to be, for a rest of only six hours is allowed between stages." The speed maintained depends upon the condition of the roads; and the number of horses furnished for each tarantass is regulated by the same factor; three horses sufficing in good weather and as many as seven being required when the roads are heavy from rain or snow.

PONIES IN INDIA.

Captain L. E. Nolan, in *Cavalry History and Tactics* (1860), gives an account of an experimental march made by 200 of the 15th Hussars from Bangalore to Hyderabad and back, 800 miles. The objects of the march were to test the capabilities of the troop horses and to ascertain if there were anything to choose between stallions and geldings in respect of endurance. To arrive at a solution of the latter question, one hundred of the men were mounted on entires and the other hundred on horses which had been castrated only six months previously, regardless of age, for the purpose of making the experiment.

The squadrons marched to their destination, took part in field-days and pageants, and started to reach Bangalore by forced marches; they accomplished the last 180 miles at a rate of thirty miles per day, bringing in only one led horse, the remainder being perfectly sound and fit for further work. One horse, a 14.3 Persian, carried a corporal who, with his accoutrements, rode 22 stone 7 lbs. It may be added that there was nothing to choose between the performances of the stallions and geldings; though the fact that the latter had so recently been castrated was held to make their achievement the more creditable.

A forced march such as this has far more value as testimony to staying power than a more trying feat performed by a single animal; but mention must be made of Captain Horne's ride. This officer, who belonged to the Madras Horse Artillery, undertook in 1841 to ride his grey Arab, "Jumping Jimmy," 400 miles in five days on the Bangalore race-course; and accomplished his task with three hours and five minutes to spare, the horse doing the last 79 miles 5 furlongs in 19 hours 55 minutes, and being quite ready for his corn when pulled up. General Tweedie, in his work on *The Arabian Horse* (1894), quotes the above particulars from the *Bengal Sporting Magazine*, in whose pages full details are given.

Captain Nolan, in the work from which quotation has been made above, sums up the shortcomings of the cavalry trooper of his day in the following pithy sentences:—

"Our cavalry horses are feeble; they measure high, but they do so from length of limb, which is weakness, not power. The blood they require is not that of our weedy race-horse (an animal more akin to the greyhound and bred for speed alone), but it is the blood of the Arab and Persian, to give them that compact form and wiry limb in which they are wanting."

The great value of the pony in India was insisted on by Mr. J. H. B. Hallen, formerly the General Superintendent of the Horse Breeding Department, in a memorandum published at Meerut in 1899. Pointing out the many spheres of utility open to the pony, he urged the local authorities and agricultural societies to foster and develop pony breeding by providing suitable stallions for public use. As proving the value of the pony, Mr. Hallen points out that in the two-wheeled cart called an *ekka*, used by the natives of Northern India, a pony will draw a load of from 4-1/2 to 6 cwt. over long distances at a rate of 5 or 6 miles an hour.

Ponies all over India are equally in request for riding and driving, and in the northern parts for pack purposes. Indeed, adds Mr. Hallen, "the pony may be said to be all round the most useful animal." The supply is not equal to the demand.

Captain H. L. Powell, R.H.A., writing in *Baily's Magazine* of March, 1900, says:—

"I am a great believer in the Arab for officers' chargers, light cavalry and mounted infantry in this campaign. The Arab is a hardy little beast, and will thrive and do well on what would be starvation rations for an ordinary troop-horse. As a rule the Arab is rather light of bone, but his bone is twice as strong as that of an underbred horse. I have an Arab pony about 14.2 which I am looking after for his owner who went out to the war, and who is now, I am sorry to say, enjoying Mr. Kruger's hospitality in Pretoria. The pony carries my 15 stone as if it was a feather, and never seems to tire."

The superiority of the Arab over the Indian country-bred is reflected in their respective cost. Mr. Hallen, in the memorandum before referred to, says stallions of the country-bred class can be obtained at from about £6 10s. to £13, while suitable Arab pony stallions cost from £16 10s. to £33.

PONIES IN NORTHERN AFRICA.[2]

The best authority on the breeds used by the Arabs of
Northern Africa is probably General E. Daumas, who held
high commands in Algeria and was for a time the French
Consul at Mascara. The Chasseurs d'Afrique are mounted
on Barbs, and thus the capabilities of these horses were of
practical importance to this officer; moreover, he took a
very keen personal interest in all matters relating to the
horse, and spared no endeavour to inform himself
concerning the breed of the country in which he resided.
Hence the description in General Daumas' book, *The
Horses of the Sahara: with Commentaries by the Emir Abd
El Kadr*(1863) is accepted as the standard on the Barb.

[2]The Barb, there is no possible doubt, is of pure Arab origin: in
the seventh century, when the Fatimite sect of Mohammedans held
sway in Egypt, numerous Arab tribes migrated to Africa and
gradually spread over the whole of the northern portion of the
continent; the horses they brought with them spread in like
manner.

The letters of the famous Emir to General Daumas,
containing categorical replies to questions put by the latter,
show that the Barbs possess endurance in a very
remarkable degree. Their average height is nowhere
mentioned in this work, but they are, as we believe,
somewhat smaller than the Arab in his native country and
in India. There is a suggestive hint of their small size in a
remark by General Daumas: he says that inexperienced
horsemen with their spurs "sometimes prick the animal on
the knee-pan and so lame him if the wound be deep."
Assuming that the average height of the horseman be 5 feet
6 inches, and making due allowance for the "straight-
legged" seat of the cavalry man, the General's remark
points to a horse certainly not over 14 hands.

In answer to General Daumas' enquiry as to the amount of
work a Barb can do, the Emir replies:—

"A horse sound in every limb and eating as much barley as
his stomach can contain can do whatever his rider can ask

of him. For this reason the Arabs say, 'give barley and over-work him,' but without tasking him over much a horse can be made to do about sixteen *parasangs* (equal to about fifty English miles) a day, day after day. It is the distance from Mascara to Koudiat Aghelizan on the Oued-Mina: it has been measured in cubits. A horse performing this journey every day, and having as much barley as it likes to eat, can go on without fatigue for three or four months without lying by a single day."

The Arabs on their *razzias*, or cattle-stealing expeditions, of necessity travel with as little encumbrance as possible: on such expeditions, which may require twenty or twenty-five days' rapid travel, each horseman carries only enough barley to give his mount eight feeds. In some parts of the Sahara green food is never given; frequent watering is recommended by all Arab horsemen.

An Arab of the Arbâa tribe gave General Daumas full particulars of a ride he once undertook to save a highly prized mare from the hands of the Turks. In twenty-four hours he rode her eighty leagues, and during the journey she obtained nothing to eat but leaves of the dwarf palm, and was watered once.

More directly bearing on our present enquiry are the particulars furnished by Colonel Duringer of the weights carried in most of the expeditions by the horses of the Chasseurs d'Afrique. These details were ascertained by the Colonel at the moment of departure of a column:—Horseman, 180 lbs.; equipment, 53 lbs.; pressed hay for five days, 55 lbs.; barley for same period, 44 lbs. The man's own provisions brought up the total burden to about 350 lbs. English = 25 stone! Daily consumption of hay and grain would reduce this colossal burden gradually; but the horse would never carry less than 16 stone 9 lbs. at the end of his journey, starting with the load described.

As regards forced marches of comparatively short duration, Colonel Duringer states that

"A good horse in the desert ought to accomplish for five or six days, one after the other, distances of 25 to 30 leagues. After a couple of days' rest, if well fed he will be quite fresh enough to repeat the feat. It is no very rare occurrence to hear of horses doing 50 or 60 leagues in twenty-four hours."

PONIES IN MOROCCO.

Mr. T. E. Cornwell, who has had twenty years' experience
of travel and residence in Morocco, gives the ponies in
common use in that country a high character as weight
carriers and for endurance on scanty food; they are also
very sure-footed. These horses he describes as Barbs, very
hardy with thick shoulders; they average 14 hands 2 inches,
rarely attaining a height of 15 hands. They generally
receive a feed of rough straw in the morning and a ration of
barley, from 6 to 7 lbs., at night; they are watered (when
water can be obtained) once a day. Grass can be had at
some seasons of the year, but the horses, being tethered
during halts, cannot graze, and as the task of cutting grass
would entail delay it is never used.

Here they come!

There they are!

On the Look Out.

On the Look Out.

Charging on them.

Receiving the Charge.

Mr. Cornwell, a 14 stone man, has ridden one of these ponies for thirty-two consecutive days, with only one day's rest, covering an average of thirty miles per day.

General Maclean, who for a long period was the "Kaid" or Commander-in-Chief of the Sultan's forces in Morocco, once tried the experiment of stabling his horses instead of picketing out in the open, which is the usual practice. The experiment did not answer, for on his next expedition every horse died; shelter for a period had no doubt rendered them susceptible to maladies brought on by exposure at night. These ponies could be purchased at a figure ranging from £8 to £11 per head. An export duty of £3 10s., which is levied on every horse sent out of Morocco, must be added to these rates by foreign purchasers.

Mr. Cornwell states that an infusion of English blood does nothing to improve these hardy Morocco ponies. Blood horses from England have been imported and crossed with the native mares, but the produce have always been leggy and less capable of continued hard work than the native breed.

PONIES IN EASTERN ASIA.

The pony commonly used in China is bred in the northern part of the country. According to a writer in *Baily's Magazine*, immense droves of ponies run on the plains three or four hundred miles from Pekin, and the breeders bring them down every year for sale in the more populous districts. They average about 13.1 in height, and though in very wretched condition when brought to market, pick up rapidly on good food. They are usually short and deep in the barrel, have good legs and feet, and fairly good shoulders. Speed is not to be expected from their conformation; but they can carry heavy weights, are of robust constitution and possess great endurance.

The Burmese ponies are smaller than the Chinese, averaging about 12 hands 2 inches, a thirteen-hand pony being considered a big one. They are generally sturdy little beasts with good shoulders, excellent bone and very strong in the back; sound, hardy and enduring, capable of doing much continuous hard work under a heavy weight on indifferent food. Like the Chinese ponies, they are somewhat slow, but they are marvellous jumpers.

Before the annexation of Upper Burma in 1885 the lower province was dependent upon the breeders of the Shan Hills and on the breeders in independent Burma for its ponies, as the export of stallions and mares was forbidden.

Since the annexation the Indian Government have sought to improve the native breed by the introduction of Arab pony stallions; the superior size and good looks of the "Indo-Burman," as the cross-bred is called, are, the writer understands, steadily leading to the disappearance of the pure Burmese. The half-bred Arab has much to recommend him over the pure Burmese pony in greater docility and speed; but these advantages appear to have been gained at some sacrifice of weight-carrying power and endurance.

Captain M. H. Hayes, in *The Points of the Horse*, states that the ponies of Sumatra, averaging about 12 hands 2 inches, are the strongest for their size he has ever seen. He describes them as "simply balls of muscle," and notes the beauty of their heads, which would seem to distinguish them as a breed from the ponies found on the mainland. The Corean pony is the smallest of Eastern breeds, but his extraordinary weight-carrying power makes him a marvel: averaging about ten hands in height and slight of build, he is nevertheless able to carry a full-grown man, on a saddle secured over a pile of rugs to atone for his small size, and to do a long day's work under a burden wholly disproportionate to his inches.

PONIES IN AUSTRALIA.

The Australian "mail-man," or mounted postman, whose duty it is to distribute and collect letters at the remote and scattered "stations" far from railway centres, prefers small horses for his arduous work, which demands endurance and speed. Thus they are described by "Australian Native" in the *Field* of June 11, 1892:—

"The mail-man's riding horse is of an entirely different class [from the pack horse which carries the bags], and is probably best described as a 'big little' animal, or a symmetrical, typical English three-quarter bred hunter of 16 to 16.2 focused into 13.2 or 13.3, with slightly higher withers, which gives the appearance of a somewhat low back."

"Bearing in mind the character of mail-men's duty, it becomes evident that of necessity their horses must possess combined stamina, high courage and speed. The stamp described have these qualities in a marked degree, and, in addition, their natural paces of jog—not an amble—and daisy-cutting canter not only enable them to get over the ground with great ease to themselves but also to their riders. Moreover, these small animals are not readily knocked up, but when they do get stale and leg-weary through extra hard work on little food, a few days on good grass is sufficient for them to regain their vitality. In Australian parlance, they are 'cut-and-come-again customers,' and unlike big horses, which, when they knock up, knock up for an indefinitely long period.

"The smartest stock horses, those in use for drafting cattle, are also small, handy and well up to 12 stone, and as their prices are the same as mail-men's nags, from £4 to £8 per head, the evidence in favour of small horses for utilitarian purposes, and also on the score of economy, preponderates. Would such small animals, withal tough and wiry, be suitable for light cavalry?"

The answer to the concluding query is undoubtedly "Yes."

PONIES IN AMERICA AND TEXAS.

The ponies of North-West America are famed for their powers of endurance, which are the more remarkable in view of their make and shape. These animals are without doubt the descendants of stock introduced by the Spaniards when they invaded Mexico early in the 16th century; the offspring of these Spanish horses in course of time spread over the whole continent.

Colonel Richard Irving Dodge remarks, in his work *Our Wild Indians* (1882), that the horses introduced by the Spaniards must have been very inferior in size, or the race has greatly degenerated; as compared with the American horse, the Indian pony is very small. As the subsequent observations of Colonel Dodge prove, these ponies, if they have lost size have lost absolutely nothing in working qualities; they have become adapted to their conditions of life and have probably gained in hardiness of constitution and endurance. He writes:—

"Averaging scarcely fourteen hands in height, the Indian pony is rather slight in build, though always having powerful fore-quarters, good legs, short, strong back, and full barrel. He has not the slightest appearance of 'blood,' though his sharp, nervous ears and bright, vicious eye indicate unusual intelligence and temper. But the amount of work he can do and the distance he can make in a specified (long) time put him fairly on a level with the Arabian or any other of the animal creation.... Treated properly, the pony will wear out two American horses, but in the hands of the Indian he is so abused and neglected that an energetic cavalry officer will wear him out."

The North-West American Indian, though a marvellous horseman as a "trick rider," has apparently no idea whatever of saving his mount, whatever the distance he has to travel. According to Colonel Dodge, who has enjoyed many opportunities of informing himself on Indian usages, more especially as an enemy, he will gallop his pony till it drops from sheer exhaustion.

As showing what a good pony can do in the hands of a man who knows how to make the most of him, Colonel Dodge states that he once tried to buy an animal which pleased his eye, offering forty dollars for it; whereupon the owner replied that the price was six hundred dollars. Repeating the incident to someone who knew the pony, he was informed that the owner had not been actuated by any boastful spirit; that he had good reason for attaching a very high value to it. The man, it appeared, had been employed to carry the mail bags between Chehuahua and El Paso, nearly 300 miles apart, during a period of six months, when the roads were closed for ordinary travel by marauding bands of Apache Indians on the watch for white men.

He had to make the perilous journey once a week, and he performed it on the pony, riding all night for three successive nights, and hiding by day. The Indians, it may be added, are deterred by superstition from risking death by night; hence an additional good reason for the express rider's choice of time to travel. For six months the pony carried him between ninety and a hundred miles on three consecutive nights in each week; he went one week and returned the next in the same way. And Colonel Dodge adds that this tax upon his powers "had not diminished the fire and flesh of that pony."

Writing of the breed in another work, *The Hunting Grounds of the Great West*, Colonel Dodge observes that civilisation spoils this pony; accustomed on the ranche and prairie to pick up his own living when turned out after a long day's work in summer, and used to semi-starvation in winter, when stabled, shod, and fed on corn, his character undergoes a change. He either becomes morose, ill-tempered, hard to manage and dangerous, or he degenerates into a fat, lazy, short-winded cob, "only fit for a baby or an octogenarian." The latter change is the more usual. We can well understand that such would be the result.

Colonel Dodge has no doubt but that the Indian pony is identical with the Texan mustang or wild horse, concerning whose qualities we may take the evidence of a contributor to the *Field*. "C. E. H." writes, in an article on "A Texas Fair," published in 1891:—

"The native stock for endurance and soundness of constitution cannot be surpassed. We have owned many of these animals of from fourteen to fifteen hands, and never had an unsound one yet. They will carry one 70 miles a day without tiring; and we sold a horse aged 8 years ten years ago, which was lately disposed of for only £3 less than the sum we then received for him."

The horses raised on the plains of Uruguay, on the River Plate, have much in common with the mustang, but retain to a greater degree the characteristics of their remote Spanish ancestry in the small lean head and well-turned limbs. They are somewhat higher than the mustang, varying between 14 and 15 hands, seldom exceeding the latter height; but the natives attach no importance to hands and inches, it being an acknowledged fact that the smallest horses are in many instances the best. Accustomed to run at large until between four and five years old, these horses are sound and hardy, capable of carrying fourteen or fifteen stone all day without tiring and able to perform hard and continuous work on little food.

ARMY HORSES OF THE FUTURE.

Let it not be supposed for a moment that in urging the merits of small horses the writer seeks to asperse the value of heavy cavalry. Weight in men and size in horses are indispensable for such work as our heavy cavalry are called upon to perform; even the civilian mind can appreciate the mysteries of tactics so far as to recognise that a charge of heavy cavalry can effect infinitely greater results upon an enemy than men mounted on ponies of fourteen hands or fourteen hands two inches.

Authorities on military affairs seem agreed that the great improvements made in small arms of precision since the Crimean War have done much to impair the former value of heavy cavalry for direct attack; it needs no trained intelligence to recognise that cavalry advancing in close rank might well be shot down to a man in attempting to charge a foe, not necessarily under cover, over a thousand yards of fairly open ground on which such a manœuvre is possible to cavalry. For artillery and transport, however, we shall always need powerful horses, and the draught power required is only to be obtained with height.

When it was made evident that very much larger numbers of mounted infantry were required for the South African campaign than had been anticipated, the remount agents were instructed to purchase cobs, and to obtain these in quantity it was necessary to go to foreign countries, the United States, Argentina, and Hungary, where they could be procured. Had the demand been made for ponies, a very large proportion of our Army's need could have been bought cheaply and quickly in this country. For in the ponies of Exmoor, Wales, the New Forest and other districts, we possess large numbers of animals whose small size bears no relation to their weight carrying power, and whose mode of life is the best possible preparation for "roughing it" in South Africa. Very different is the case with the animals shipped from England.

For generations, now, horses for the saddle and lighter draught work have been very largely bred less as necessaries than luxuries; the conditions of their lives are artificial in a high degree, and the constitution which could formerly withstand exposure, hard and continuous work and scanty feed, has been softened by pampering. To take such horses out of their stables where the temperature is regulated, where they are warmly clothed and regularly fed, and despatch them to endure the hardships of campaigning in countries where hay and oats are unknown or unprocurable, and the forage obtainable is unsuited to English chargers—in short, to most severely tax their powers under a set of conditions entirely opposed to those to which they are accustomed—is to invite heavy mortality.

The sacrifice of useful qualities to the "god of inches" is deplored only in so far as it applies to horses for mounted infantry and light cavalry. The utility of large and powerful horses is not, and never has been, questioned. In point of fact it is their value for the work in which they are employed that has done something to blind us to the very real value—for special tasks—of ponies: and if the foregoing pages do anything to prove that there is in modern warfare a place of the highest importance which can only be filled by the small horse of 14.2 or thereabouts, their object has been fulfilled.

BREEDING SMALL HORSES.

Assuming that the peculiar suitability of horses between 14 hands and 14 hands 3 inches for mounted infantry and light cavalry purposes is acknowledged by the authorities, and that these forces will in future form a larger proportion of our standing army, it behoves us to turn our attention to the task of breeding. The high prices obtainable for first-class polo ponies have given a stimulus to pony-breeding, and it may be said the foundations of the industry have been laid. What the present remount market is to the breeder of hunters, so may the market for mounted infantry cobs be to the breeder of polo ponies; but with this difference, that the latter, being handicapped by the height limit of 14 hands 2 inches, and the exceedingly high standard of merit[3] required by polo players, will have a larger proportion of "misfits." To compensate for the paucity of valuable prizes he may hope to draw in the lottery of breeding, both stock and maintenance will be cheaper, if the business be conducted on the lines which seem best calculated to result in production of the horse desired.

[3]See *Ponies Past and Present*, by Sir Walter Gilbey, Bart. Vinton & Co., Ltd.

What is required is an animal between 14.0 and 14.3 hands; it must be stout and able to carry weight, capable of covering long distances at fair speed, able to subsist on coarse or poor food for weeks together without losing condition, strong of constitution to withstand the exposure inevitable on a campaign, and the more tractable the better. To get small horses endowed with these qualifications we must look to the breeds which possess them in marked degree, to the ponies of the Welsh Hills, Exmoor, the New Forest, the Fell districts, and West of Ireland. In these we have ponies ranging in height from 12.2 to 13.3 or 14 hands; they are compact, sturdy, and untiring; they can carry weights which are out of all ratio to their size; they live on grass, and the open-air life they lead, year in year out, has made them completely independent of the luxurious "coddling" bestowed upon other horses.

These ponies lack only the size required in our mounted infantry horse, and these essentials we can obtain from the sire we shall select. Keeping ever in mind that an animal of the polo-pony stamp—a hunter in miniature—is required, what sire is more likely to get the desired pony than the Arab? We might use a small Thoroughbred with excellent results, but having regard to the rarity with which we find good bone and sound constitution in the Thoroughbred, and also having regard to the inherent soundness and stoutness of the Eastern horse, we shall probably obtain more satisfactory young stock from Forest and Moorland dams if we use the Arab sire. Blood, it is truly urged, gives the superior speed and courage required in the polo-pony, but let us not forget that Arabs were the sires from which all our modern race-horses are descended. The best horses on the Turf to-day may be traced to one of the three famous sires—the Byerly Turk imported in 1689, the Darley Arabian in 1706, and the Godolphin Arabian in 1730: all of them, it may be remarked, horses under 14 hands.

By going back to the original strain we shall obtain all the useful qualities our Thoroughbreds possess without those undesired characteristics, greatly increased size, great speed, delicacy of constitution and complete inability to lead a natural life which man's long-maintained endeavours to breed race horses have implanted in them. In a word, we shall obtain a natural and not an artificial horse; the modern race-horse is practically everything the mounted infantry cob must not be, saving only in respect of speed, and speed for only a short distance is of no great use to mounted infantry. By using the Arab we may expect to obtain the qualities our race horses boasted a century and a half or two centuries ago, when they stood 14 hands to 14.3—the famous Gimcrack is said to have measured 14 hands 0-1/4 inch.

There is much to be said in favour of the policy of returning to the original Eastern stock to find suitable sires for our proposed breed of ponies. While we have been breeding the Thoroughbred for speed and speed only, Arab breeders have continued to breed for stoutness, endurance and good looks. By going to Arab stock for our sires we might at the beginning sacrifice some measure of speed: but what was lost in that respect would be more than compensated by the soundness of constitution and limb which are such conspicuous traits in the Eastern horse. Furthermore, the difficulty of size which confronts us in the Thoroughbred sire is much diminished if we adopt the Arab as our foundation sire.

By crossing the Arab on mares of our forest and moorland breeds we shall obtain the increased size and speed required, while it will be possible to preserve the valuable qualities of the dam. Those qualities, the hardiness, robustness of constitution, sureness of foot, and ability to thrive on poor feed, are the natural outcome of the conditions under which they have lived for centuries; and to preserve them in the young stock, it will be necessary to rear the cross-bred foals under conditions as nearly natural as their constitution will allow. What those conditions should be circumstances must determine; but it is possible to combine large measure of liberty with a certain amount of shelter from the rigours of winter, such as the foal with Arab blood in his veins would require. To take up the young stock as soon as weaned, stable and feed them artificially, though this course would preserve them from the risks of exposure, would produce failure in other directions. It would encourage undue physical development while undermining that capacity for endurance of hardship which is so essential.

From a drawing on stone by Gauci.

GIMCRACK

Whether, by careful attention to mating and management, it would be possible to establish a breed of small horses as a fixed type is a question only prolonged experience will be able to answer. It is quite certain that we shall never be able to reckon on getting stock which, when fully grown and furnished, will neither exceed nor fall short of the limit of 14 hands 2 inches, at which the breeder will aim with the prizes of the polo pony market in his mind's eye. But there is sound reason to think that we can build upon an Arab and Forest or Moorland pony foundation a breed of small horses such as we need for mounted infantry.

There are difficulties in the way; and not the least is the peculiar care and watchfulness that must be exercised in order to hit the "happy medium" between artificial life, with its attendant drawbacks of probable overgrowth and certain delicacy of constitution, and the free, natural existence, which may prove fatal to the cross-bred youngsters and will certainly check their growth.

Having shown the great utility of small horses for work requiring endurance, hardiness, and weight-carrying power, as proved by the writings of authorities who, in several instances, employed them merely because they could procure no other animals, and learned what their qualities are by experience, we may briefly summarise what has been said in regard to the foundation stock we possess.

(1) The pony dams of our Forest and Moorland breeds cannot be surpassed.

(2) The sire chosen should be a *small* thoroughbred or an Arab. If a half-breed sire is used his dam should be one not less than three parts thoroughbred.

(3) Inasmuch as the forest and moorland ponies owe their small size and soundness to the hardships of the free and

natural conditions in which they live, their half-bred produce should—

(*a*) Lead a similarly free and natural life as far as climate permits, in order to inure them to the hardships of warfare and general work:

(*b*) Should exist, as far as possible, on natural herbage: as in all cases artificial feeding tends to render them less hardy and enduring.

APPENDIX.

Since this little book was placed in the printers' hands, a work published in 1836 has come under the writer's notice. This is entitled *A Comparative View of the Form and Character of the English Racer and Saddle Horse during the Past and Present Centuries.*[4] It was written with the view of showing that the natural qualities of the horse— endurance, weight-carrying power and speed maintained over long distances, are found at their best in the horse which has been reared under natural conditions and whose stature has not been increased by "selection" in breeding and by artificial conditions of life. In the opening words of the Introductory chapter;

[4]Illustrated by eighteen plates of horses.—Anon. Published by Thomas Hookham, London.

"The main object of these pages is to investigate the results of that structural enlargement of animals which is unnatural, to point out those properties which may be acquired by certain of them when fully reclaimed, and those which they are likely to lose in this condition.

"The natural stature both of horses and cattle is small compared with that which they acquire when domesticated. The enlargement of their structure is effected by grass made by art unnaturally rich, or by food yet more foreign to their nature. Supplied plentifully with either throughout the year, horses acquire an increase of stature in muscular power which enables them to carry or drag a heavier weight...."

The author proceeds to observe that in enlarging the structure we seem to modify rather than improve the vital powers of the animal; and by way of illustrating his meaning points out with great truth that—

"In the human race any extent of skeleton or amount of muscle which is unusually large is rarely allied with a full amount of vital power. Still, the man who has most muscle can make the greatest muscular exertion. If we change the nature of the trial and render it one of time or privations, the greater vital power of smaller but well-formed men is apparent."

Our author then proceeds to examine the properties which animals derive from nature, comparing these with those they derive from art. In this connection I have been much interested to observe that he cites the greater strength, staying power and activity of the hare of the downs over the hare of the park and low pasture-land. The same comparison was made by me[5] as proof of the advantages to an animal of life-conditions that compel the free use of limbs.

[5]"Young Race Horses," pp. 21-2, by Sir Walter Gilbey, Bart. Vinton & Co., Limited, 1898.

Nature, observes this author, erects her own standard for measuring the constitutional power of her creatures, and the individuals who no longer come up to this perish prematurely. In other words, the constitutional strength of animals is so regulated by, and adjusted to, the conditions of feed and climate under which those animals pass their lives, that they thrive vigorously. We do not, for instance, find the ponies of the Welsh hills or of Exmoor, a feeble and delicate race; the feeble individuals die off without perpetuating their weaknesses, and those which come up to the standard of vitality Nature has prescribed survive to reproduce their kind.

The following, which has direct bearing on the subject matter of the foregoing pages, must be noted:—

"Many facts have been recorded showing the extraordinary power of ponies for travelling fast and far, but these are so well known as to make it unnecessary to specify them here."

Nevertheless on a subsequent page we find recorded a very striking example of endurance, which compares favourably with any of those quoted in the foregoing pages and in my little work on Ponies:[6]

[6]"Ponies: Past and Present." By Sir Walter Gilbey, Bart Vinton & Co., Ltd.

"The late Mr. Allen of Sudbury, in Suffolk, often during the course of his life rode from that place to London and back (112 miles) in the course of a day upon a pony. This task was performed by several which Mr. Allen had in succession. When he returned home from these expeditions he was in the habit of turning the little animal he had ridden at once into the lanes without giving it a grain of corn. Mr. Allen, whose weight was very light, rode at a smart canter. He always selected Welsh ponies, saying that no others were so stout."

The author adds that if any one of our enlarged horses could be found capable of performing this task it would certainly not be on a grass diet; which is undoubtedly true.

At the date this book was published, 1836, the deterioration which our race horses had undergone through the abolition of long-distance races was a subject of comment. The author deplores the altered conditions of the Royal Plates and the feebleness of the horses bred only for speed, on the ground that the change was producing ill effects upon all saddle-horses.

The author puts the whole case for a changed method of breeding in a nutshell when he writes that "we want a class of horses bred under a system which holds the balance even between speed, stoutness and structural power." As proving that the balance can be struck, he points to the uniformity of speed and stoutness which distinguishes a good pack of foxhounds. None are markedly faster than the others; the aim is to get the hounds as even in all respects as possible, and there are numerous packs which prove to us that this aim can be achieved with wonderful completeness. It goes without saying, however, that it is infinitely easier to build up a level pack of hounds than it would be to develop a given number of horses all of which shall be alike!

It is exceedingly interesting to find that sixty-four years ago
this author, with the improvement of horses in view, should
advocate adoption of the step which has been urged in the
chapter (p. 36 and *seq.*) on "Breeding Small Horses." He is
in favour of a National Establishment or breeding stud, but
that is a detail; he explains that his only reason for making
it a Government department is to secure that continuity of
policy which is otherwise unattainable. The nucleus of his
scheme is to "obtain from the East a considerable number
of well selected ponies. The better portion would be found
to possess much natural speed, stoutness under severe
exertion, with limbs and feet peculiarly adapted for moving
rapidly on a hard surface." The persons commissioned to
buy these ponies

"Would search in vain for these properties which are
acquired under a system of continued selection. Looking
only for natural qualities, they should select animals as
nearly in a state of nature as they could find them; having
good symmetry, a full amount of muscle and whatever
natural speed the best animals of the best race are found to
possess."

He would have these horses tested for speed when brought
home, the standard being a natural degree of speed and not
that of the Turf.

"The offspring of these small horses should be tried in each
succeeding generation; and we should be satisfied for a few
years to see the natural speed of the race gradually
augment, retaining only for breeding such as went through
their trials satisfactorily."

On a later page he suggests the propriety of crossing these
Eastern sires with our Forest and Moorland ponies. He
cannot doubt that the immediate offspring of the first cross
will prove suitable for the saddle:

"The best saddle horses we possess being now occasionally
produced by crossing the race horse with a pony mare. This
experiment often succeeding with one of the parents so ill
fitted for taking part in it as the modern racer, there is every

reason to conclude that, with parents properly constituted
on both sides, the breeding of the best class of saddle
horses might be accompanied with little uncertainty."

Thus far we find that the suggestions for breeding small
horses set out on pp. 36-43 were anticipated over sixty
years ago. We must, before taking leave of the author,
glance at his plan for "renovating" our half wild breeds of
ponies. If it were practicable to carry out the experiment he
outlines, the results would be of undoubted interest.

"To experiment properly in this matter it is necessary that a
public establishment should appropriate some extensive
district of unreclaimed and bad pasturage to the
maintenance of a large body of ponies. These should be
interfered with only to the extent of severe selection,
founded on annual trials; taking the animals for this
purpose from their pasturage for a few days during the
summer, and tying them to pickets. Here they should be
closely inspected, and after the best formed had been
selected from the rest, they should be taken ten or twenty at
a time by rough riders of light weight, and submitted to a
trial of some hours' duration. The animals which went
through this satisfactorily should be divided into two
portions: one should be returned to their old pasturage to
remain at their then stature; while the other portion should
be made to occupy a somewhat better pasturage in order
that their offspring might acquire greater stature, the rest to
be drafted and sold. When old enough the enlarged stock
should be tried, and such as went through it well should be
kept, and turned out into a little better pasturage than that in
which they had been reared, while those rejected should be
drafted and sold. It is only in this very gradual manner that
the stature of a race can be increased to the point required.
Ponies of a pure race being so vigorous as to be wholly
unfitted for rich pasturage, they become upon it balls of fat.
None of our native ponies under the plan now proposed
would be enlarged or withdrawn from their miserable
pasturage unless their form and action were good; the only
change then effected would be a pasturage a little better.
Any further enlargement would be made to depend upon

the manner in which they had been found to bear the preceding one."

His plan has at all events the great merit that it proposes to seek the limit of enlargement in the half-wild ponies without risking loss of hardiness and other valuable qualities by pampering.

www.ingramcontent.com/pod-product-compliance
Lightning Source LLC
Chambersburg PA
CBHW070233290526
45789CB00004B/1605